SWASTIKA
AT WAR

SWASTIKA AT WAR

A photographic record of the war in Europe as seen by the cameramen of the German magazine *Signal*

PICTURES SELECTED BY ROBERT HUNT
TEXT BY TOM HARTMAN

Doubleday & Company Inc
Garden City, New York

Introduction

Photographs © The Robert Hunt Library 1975
Text © T. R. Hartman 1975

ISBN 0 385 11150 9

Library of Congress Catalog Card
Number 75–4164
All rights reserved
Doubleday edition 1975

Printed in Great Britain by
Ebenezer Baylis and Son Ltd
Worcester and London

Signal is generally considered to have been the most spectacular publication to appear during the Second World War, yet all that now remain are the few volumes of file copies carefully preserved in various museums and archives. Nevertheless, during its brief lifetime *Signal* had a tremendous effect not only upon its enormous readership but upon the magazine publishing world itself, an effect that is still felt today.

The name of the 'father' of *Signal* has hitherto remained unpublished, but it can now be revealed that he was in fact Doctor Paul Leverkuehn, whose earlier career is of some interest in relation to the conception of *Signal*. In the First World War he served with the intelligence unit of Colonel Nicolai in the Middle East, in the campaign immortalized by T. E. Lawrence. In 1923 he joined the Foreign Office and was sent to Washington to take part in negotiations concerning the return of confiscated German property and the relaxation of reparations payments. From 1930 until 1939 he worked as a lawyer in Berlin, but was drafted to the German High Command on the outbreak of war, where, with Colonel Blau, he was responsible for Wehrmacht propaganda abroad. There he conceived the idea of *Signal*, and the first magazine appeared in April 1940. The title of the magazine was carefully chosen, the word 'signal' being much the same in most European languages.

Dr Leverkuehn's association with his brainchild did not last long, for he was soon posted once again to the Middle East. His subsequent career is less relevant; suffice it here to say that he survived the war to become a CDU member of the Bundestag and died in 1960.

Signal was now born and was certainly a most privileged child. For *Signal* there were no financial worries or paper shortages; all was at once made available to this highly effective propaganda weapon, dedicated to maintaining the prestige of the Wehrmacht. Thanks to a team of 150 translators, the magazine was in its heyday printed in over 20 languages, and the print run at one time reached nearly 2·5 million. The printing was distributed throughout Europe wherever the necessary facilities were available. Nor was there any restriction on the availability of editorial staff. The nucleus of the team had worked together for some years before the war at Ullstein, a distinguished German publishing house, and others were drafted in as occasion demanded. At least half the editors belonged to army propaganda units and, as such, held military rank. But it is interesting to note that nearly all the writers, scientists and journalists who co-operated in the production of *Signal* have, since the war, continued to work in the same field and their subsequent objective criticism of the political scene seems to indicate that it is unlikely that they were deeply committed or convinced party members.

In addition to their own writing, *Signal's* editorial team also had access to the bulletins issued by the 1,500 official reporters covering every branch of the armed forces on all fronts. But, for all the talent of the editorial staff, it is the photographs in *Signal* which still grip us today and which justify the publication of this handsome book. The editors had at their disposal the skills of more than 1,000 cameramen working for the propaganda units of the army, the navy and the air force. In addition, there were special photographers whose permits gave them immediate access to any form of transport at any time on any front. Provided with the very latest equipment in a field of scientific technique in which Germany had always led the world, their greatest advantage lay in the generous use of colour film, in those days still very rare. I recall particularly the names of the photographers Arthur Grimm, Hans Hubmann, Dietrich Kenneweg, Hilmar Pabel, Wolfgang Weber and Benno Wundshammer.

The overall policy of *Signal* was set by the OKW/Wpt, in consultation with the Ministry of Propaganda and the Foreign Office, but if the general direction of the magazine was controlled from above, it was left to the editorial staff to implement it. As the war progressed and the belligerents continued to grow in number, greater emphasis was placed upon the need to defend Europe against the menace of communism. Antisemitic tirades remained throughout an obligation imposed from above, and the editors, perfectly aware that the magazine was primarily a weapon in the propaganda war, had no choice but to obey. Nevertheless we tried as best we could in indirect ways, and often at considerable risk, to demolish the barriers of racial and class hatred, to prick the bubble of chauvinistic arrogance and to destroy the myth of the master race. Today the casual reader of old copies of *Signal* may find this hard to believe, but those who were grown up at the time and who care to read a little between the lines will not, I think, dispute this contention.

The general quality of the articles, in both content and style, was extremely high and the standard of production, particularly in the use of colour printing, was years ahead of anything else in the field at that time. It can be truthfully said that, as a result, *Signal* had an enormous effect throughout wartime Europe. For all of us who were associated with it I am happy that our work is not altogether forgotten, and I hope that those who read this book will agree that *Signal's* photographers did a very remarkable job indeed.

GUNTHER HEYSING
Former Deputy Editor of *Signal*

1940

At the beginning of April, 1940, when the first number of Signal appeared, the war was already seven months old. The British Expeditionary Force was still in North-Eastern France and the stalemate which history knows as the Phoney War had yet to be broken. Prior to the outbreak of war Germany had occupied Austria and Czechoslovakia, acts of blatant aggression which at the time had gone unchallenged by Britain or France. However, the invasion of Poland on 1 September, 1939, finally provoked the Allies into retaliation and Great Britain and France declared war on Germany two days later. But neither materially nor geographically were the Allies in a position to go to the aid of Poland and by the end of the month the country had been partitioned between Russia and Germany, the two having signed a non-aggression pact the previous month, by a secret clause in which this act of territorial rape had been agreed upon.

Italy, though friendly to Germany, remained neutral, as did all other European countries, while on land the belligerents faced each other, without coming to blows, throughout the winter of 1939-40.

This situation lasted until April, 1940. Hitler was undisputed master of most of Central Europe and only Britain and France stood against him. They were soon to learn that his greed was far from satisfied.

A German searchlight crew on the watch for enemy aircraft. The searchlight is linked to a sound locator which determines the position of the aircraft from the noise of its engines and to an ack-ack battery whose guns follow the beam of the searchlight.

The Phoney War ended on 9 April, 1940 when Germany invaded Denmark and Norway. Germany had been prepared to tolerate Scandinavian neutrality so long as she had exclusive access to the Swedish iron-ore supplies which were shipped through Narvik and then south down the Norwegian coast to Germany. But in the light of intelligence reports that the Allies were intending to disrupt this traffic Hitler sanctioned the invasion of Denmark and Norway. Allied intervention, as we shall see, proved ineffective, and this further act of aggression not only secured his northern flank against encroachment through the Baltic but also enabled him to establish bases on the Norwegian coast from which to reinforce his naval and air offensive against Britain. The caption to this picture, taken somewhere in Denmark, reads "Machine Gun up front ! Soon a steel greeting will be sent to the enemy." These are ordinary Wehrmacht troops ; the man on the left carries an M.34 machine gun.

Although the caption to this picture reads, "A damned close shot. Luckily heads were lowered in time", the evidence suggests that it is in fact a training picture taken in Germany.

Above: The Junkers Ju 87 was usually known as the Stuka, although the word is actually a contraction of the German for dive-bomber and could be applied to any aircraft employed in that role. The Ju 87 was remarkably successful, when used in conjunction with ground troops, at softening up the enemy and played a major role in the Blitzkrieg advances of the early part of the War. But it was later to prove no match for experienced pilots flying the faster and more manoeuvrable British and American fighters. On the left can be seen one of the Ju 87's three 7.9mm machine guns. It had a maximum speed of 238mph.

Right: On 10 May, 1940, Hitler launched his western offensive and met with no more resistance than he had encountered in Poland the previous autumn. Holland fell in four days and Belgium surrendered on 28 May. This picture is captioned, "The rider of modern times. Rolling over everything and spitting destruction. Panzers smooth out the path to victory." This is a Panzer Mark IV with a short 75mm gun and was the heaviest tank then used by the German army. The commander is wearing the old-style black Panzer uniform with the large beret to hide the crash-helmet beneath.

Left: This picture was taken in Holland probably on the 12th or 13th of May. Heavy air attacks, combined with paratroop landings and massive armoured thrusts on the ground soon overcame all resistance and the country capitulated on the 14th. Anxious that the Dutch should not waste time in reaching their decision the Germans had that morning bombarded the centre of Rotterdam, destroying 25,000 houses in 4 hours. The caption reads, ''The enemy has installed itself in a farm and dominates the road, but a gun is brought forward, the walls collapse in a cloud of dust, the enemy is silenced and the advance continues.''

Right: Meanwhile in Norway the German steamroller had also flattened all resistance. By 8th June the Allied forces, amounting to some 24,000 French, British and Polish troops, had been evacuated and the country settled down to four years in the twilight of the Nazi régime. One immediate effect of the disastrous allied intervention in Norway was the resignation of Mr Chamberlain as Prime Minister of Great Britain and his replacement by Mr Winston Churchill. Here, somewhere on the Norwegian coast, German soldiers, on the lookout for enemy aircraft, man 20mm Light ack-ack guns.

Above: Following the German invasion of Holland and Belgium, the French and British, who had hitherto been obliged to observe the neutrality of the Low Countries, were at once called to their aid. It was, of course, too late, and Dutch resistance was overcome in four days. However, the Allies had advanced swiftly through Belgium and the Germans were faced with the first serious opposition they had so far encountered. There was heavy fighting on the Meuse, in the Ardennes and along the Albert Canal. But on 13 May the Germans struck through the Ardennes with about 1000 heavy tanks and on the evening of the 14th Sedan was evacuated. The caption reads, "Sedan in flames. After the German occupation French artillery bombarded the town, setting whole streets on fire."

Below: These French prisoners-of-war are described as "an assortment of the coloured races of the earth."

Above: German infantry made much use of dinghies to get across the many rivers which flow through Belgium and North-Eastern France.

A dramatic picture of a
French town in the final
agony of its subjugation.
The text reads : "The
opponent had changed the
city into a fortress.
Throughout an entire
morning it stopped the
advance of the Germans.
Each house was a firmly-
held position, larded with
machine-guns and men
who held the streets with a
murderous fire. Then death
came from the air. Stukas
swarmed down with the
screams of sirens ; shells of
all calibres rained upon it.
Shattered roofs and walls
broke the will of the
garrison. Flames shot out
of the holes which had
once been windows.
Rubbish piled up and
blackened timberwork
blocked the streets. The
enemy is thrown back ; the
city is in German hands.
The picture shows
particularly clearly that the
war raged only over the
heavily defended lines of
retreat of the enemy.
Houses surrounding these
streets remain completely
intact " !

Above: A German 21cm gun. This type of heavy artillery was mounted on rolling stock and used to bombard such vital targets as munition depots, railway junctions, important road intersections and assembly points of troops.

Top right: After 14 May the British and French forces were driven steadily back. The Germans, advancing south from Brussels, which they entered on 17 May, broke through the French line between Sedan and Valenciennes and turned west towards the Channel ports. The B.E.F. was still putting up a stubborn fight further north when on 28 May came the news of the capitulation of Belgium. Evacuation was now the only solution and how many could be rescued the only question. That so few were lost bears witness to the enduring miracle of Dunkirk. Here a German camera crew records the evidence of the British disaster. The shattered remains of some British Army lorries can be seen in the background.

Bottom right: The text says, "An impressive scene of the British catastrophe at Dunkirk — the state of an enemy battleship after an attack by Stukas." It is certainly impressive but is in fact the French destroyer, *Bourvasque*.

Left: After the evacuation of the B.E.F. the demoralized French armies faced the Germans alone and the only question that remained to be answered was how long they would hold out before accepting the inevitable. The caption says, "Day by day the circle round Paris tightens," and must, therefore, have been taken on about 12 June.

Below left: The French having destroyed all road-signs, these reconnaissance men had to rely on their map-reading skills to show the troops the way.

Below: The Germans entered Paris on 14 June, 1940. Here exhausted troops are seen riding into the city on a gun limber.

Above: Exhibiting a more suitably martial air, trumpeters sound a fanfare as the German victory parade passes the Arc de Triomphe.

Right: The Victory Parade passes along the Avenue Foch.

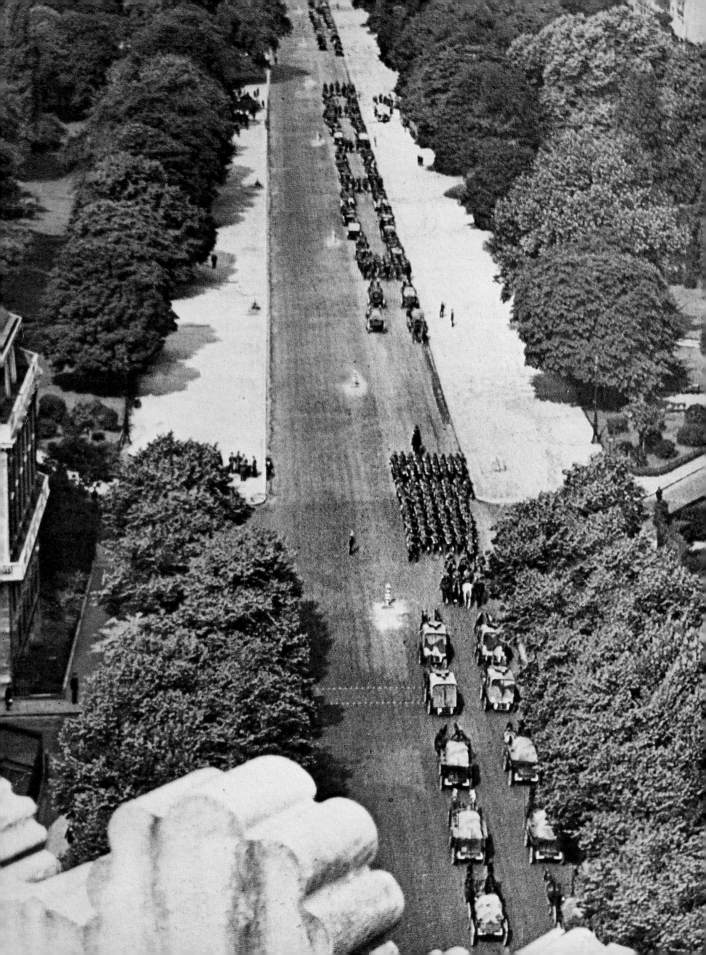

Left: The aged Marshal Pétain, having succeeded Paul Reynaud as head of the French Government on 16 June, at once negotiated terms of surrender with Hitler by which the Germans occupied the whole of Northern France and all the western seaboard. Pétain established a puppet government at Vichy, in unoccupied France, but he was only the nominal head. In reality it was controlled by the Germans with the active co-operation of Pierre Laval. The speed with which the Germans overran France was due in no small measure to the ability of their engineers to throw an improvised bridge across a river in the shortest possible time. Here a horse-drawn 10.5cm gun crosses a pontoon bridge somewhere in the now occupied part of Northern France.

Above: Having thrown the British out of France, Hitler now started making plans for the invasion of England. This was code-named 'Operation Sealion' and its success, as Hitler rightly appreciated, would depend upon the Germans first achieving a state of indisputable superiority both at sea and in the air. To this end a massive aerial bombardment of Britain was planned, which would so demoralize the enemy that all further resistance would crumble. Here a German freighter, which had been sunk by the British, is used as a target by German bomber crews preparing for the raids to come.

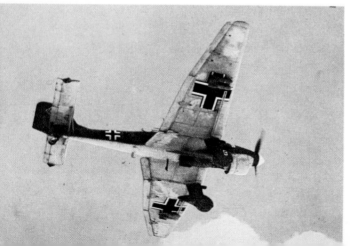

A remarkable series of photographs of Ju 87s taken, according to *Signal* on a bombing raid over England in the summer of 1940. However it seems unlikely that this was the case since the fields look more continental in pattern and by this time the Stuka had become almost obsolescent, having proved no match for even the slowest of the British fighters.

Above: The Battle of Britain lasted from July to September, 1940, and cost the Germans nearly twice as many aircraft as it did the British. The Ju 87 could carry one 1100lb bomb or one 550lb bomb and four of 110lbs. Here a 550lb bomb is being stowed.

Above: Messerschmitt Bf 110s over England.

Over: The fall of France left Germany in control of the coastline of Europe from the North Cape to the Pyrenees. While this gave her the supreme advantage of having numerous bases from which to harass Allied shipping in the North Sea and the Atlantic, at the same time it placed a heavy burden on her coastal defence resources. Here high speed minesweepers are seen on a coastal patrol.

The Messerschmitt Bf 110 was originally designed as a long-range bomber destroyer but was used as an escort fighter during the Battle of Britain, in which role it proved a failure due to its poor manoeuvrability when faced with the much nimbler single-engined Hurricanes and Spitfires. It was later used as a night fighter and light bomber. The original caption is worth reprinting : ''Here on the white edge of England's chalk coast ran the route of the British convoys. Here, however, German fighters and bombers struck day and night until England's eastern ports were closed to traffic. In tough combat the German Air Force has won total freedom of action.''

The caption to this picture reads as follows :
"In the cloud-covered English skies it is the same story
every day. A Messerschmitt has discovered a Spitfire and
turns towards it. The hunter becomes the hunted. The
RAF pilot banks down and away, trying to escape ; but the
Messerschmitt stays with him, gains on him and peppers
him with machine gun fire until he crashes." Not only is
that a somewhat one-sided view of the Battle of Britain,
in which the Germans eventually lost 1389 aircraft to the
British 792, but the picture itself is a fake. The markings on
the wings of the Spitfire are in the wrong place and the
colours on the tail are in the wrong order. Presumably the
Germans decided to patch up a Spitfire which had crash-
landed in Europe and use it for propaganda photographs
such as this.

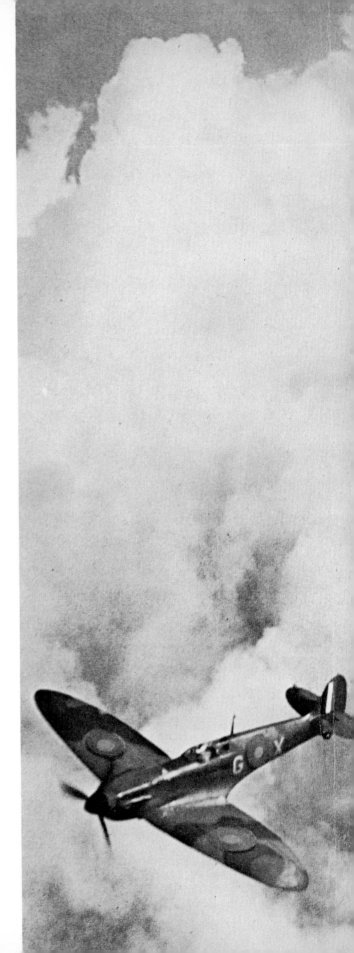

Since 1922 Benito Mussolini, the founder of the Fascist movement, had ruled Italy as a virtual dictator, but his visions of territorial aggrandisement in Europe were thwarted by the rise of Hitler; for although Mussolini had been in power for 11 years when the former became Chancellor of Germany, thereafter it soon became apparent that Hitler was the more powerful of the two and Mussolini was obliged to divert his attention from Austria and satisfy his dreams of empire elsewhere. As he said "My object is simple. I want to make Italy great, respected and feared." So in 1935 he invaded Ethiopia, an act of barefaced and criminal aggression to which the Allies chose to turn a blind eye. As *Punch* put it, under a cartoon entitled "The Awful Warning":
*We don't want you to fight,
But, by jingo, if you do,
We shall probably issue a
joint memorandum
suggesting a mild
disapproval of you.*
Unimpressed by the disapproval of the Allies, Mussolini decided to match the German occupation of Czechoslovakia in March, 1939 by annexing Albania and in May the two Fascist powers signed a treaty in Berlin which Mussolini christened the Pact of Steel. Nevertheless he waited until 10 June, 1940, when the fall of France was assured, before throwing in his lot with Hitler and declaring war on Britain and France. These pictures, which appeared in the August issue of *Signal*, were clearly intended to convey the message "Welcome to the Club."

1941

At the end of 1940 Britain still stood alone but, as Churchill said: "We may, I am sure, rate this tremendous year as the most splendid, as it was the most deadly, year in our long English and British story . . . We had not flinched or wavered. We had not failed. The soul of the British people and race had proved invincible . . . Alone, but upborne by every generous heartbeat of mankind, we had defied the tyrant in the height of his triumph."

The German Air Force had been repulsed. The threat of invasion, though still very real, was receding. The wheels of industry were turning smoothly and with ever increasing speed, and drawn together by gratitude for their delivery and pride in their achievement, the people of Britain stood united against the enemy.

The war in North Africa began on 13 September, 1940, when the Italians invaded Egypt, but little mention is to be found of it in *Signal* since at this stage it was a purely Anglo-Italian affair. The close of the year found General O'Connor in the middle of his dramatic drive to the West, in the course of which, in a period of two months, he advanced 500 miles, took 130,000 prisoners, 400 tanks and 850 pieces of artillery. However the fortunes of war in North Africa were soon to take a dramatic turn with the arrival, on 12 February, of General Erwin Rommel, the Desert Fox.

One is bound to think that the late Walt Disney would not have been very pleased to learn that "Peg-Leg Pete" had been conscripted into the Italian Air Force!
These airmen were stationed in France to fly bombing raids over England, but they suffered such heavy casualties that they were soon switched to other duties.

Above: Until the arrival of General Rommel in North Africa the British had had things very much their own way. But in January, 1941, Hitler decided to go to the aid of his less martial allies and on 12 February Rommel landed at Tripoli, soon to be followed by two divisions (the 5th Light Motorized and the 15th Panzer), known to history as the Afrika Korps. Rommel at once took the offensive and by the end of April, with the exception of the beleaguered garrison at Tobruk, all British forces had been driven out of Cyrenaica and back into Egypt. The picture shows a Bf 110 landing in the desert.

Left: The pilot of a Bf 109 gets ready for take-off.

Above: A 'silhouette' of General Rommel driving through the desert in his command car. At this time (June, 1941) activity in the North African campaign was at a relatively low ebb since Rommel's rapid eastward advance from Tripoli had stretched his lines of communication to their utmost limit.

Left: ''Shells across the Channel'' reads the caption. But by May, 1941, when this picture appeared, Hitler had abandoned his plans for the invasion of England and was concentrating his attention on the imminent invasion of Russia.

Above: As in North Africa, so in the Balkans, the Germans were obliged to come to the assistance of the Italians. Italy, having occupied Albania in April, 1939, used that country as a base from which to invade Greece in October, 1940. But the Greeks fought back with bitter determination and so, on 6 April, 1941, the Germans, who had occupied Bulgaria in the previous month, marched on into Greece, at the same time cutting through Southern Yugoslavia to join up with the Italians in Albania. The result was never in doubt and Athens fell on 27 April. Of some 60,000 British, Commonwealth and Allied troops then in the country, over 50,000 were safely evacuated.

The picture shows a column of German troops marching through Greece.

Right: "Not a breath of wind disturbs the dry brush. The hot air smells of sand and petrol while the metal of the great bird creaks from time to time in the scorching sun." Clearly the writer of this caption had a vivid imagination. The "great bird" is a Messerschmitt Bf 110. The time is June, 1941, in which month the British made an unsuccessful bid to relieve the beleaguered garrison of Tobruk. The operation, codenamed "Battleaxe," was a failure and shortly afterwards General Auchinleck replaced General Wavell as Commander of the British and Commonwealth troops in North Africa.

Previous page: At the same time the Germans were advancing rapidly through Yugoslavia. As the caption says "The campaign in Serbia lasted twelve days, at the end of which an army of 1.4 million men acknowledged their total defeat." The dates were : Invasion − 6 April ; occupation of Belgrade − 13 April ; capitulation − 17 April. Here a column of German tanks confronts a column of Serbian lorries. The vehicle in the left foreground is a half-track.

Above: Having failed to batter the British into submission by aerial bombardment, Hitler issued a directive on 8 February, 1941, in which he emphasized the importance of attacking merchant marine traffic bound for British ports. The ensuing offensive became known as the Battle of the Atlantic and one of the most potent single forces in the battle was the German heavy cruiser *Hipper,* seen here at her anchorage at Brest. Churchill has this to say about the *Hipper's modus operandi* : "Meanwhile the *Hipper* had fallen upon a homeward-bound Sierra Leone convoy near the Azores which had not yet been joined by

an escort. In a savage attack lasting an hour she destroyed seven out of nineteen ships, making no attempt to rescue survivors, and regained Brest two days later."

Right: There was little activity in the desert during the latter half of 1941, and while both sides concentrated on perfecting their lines of supply, *Signal's* caption writer gave himself whole-heartedly to the cause of German propaganda : "Sun, tornadoes and scorpions. Beneath the blazing sun the unending to and fro of the big supply planes, loaded with supplies for weapons and vehicles, with ammunition, food and medical stores, and, above all, with petrol and water. The sand-storms, which often rise to a height of 6000 feet, are part of the daily life to which the crews have become accustomed, as they have also to the unremitting heat, the scorpions in the sand and the British fighters who try to intercept them. The endless chain of the faithful supply crews reaches without respite across the loneliness of the desert" ! The aircraft with red bosses are Messerschmitt Bf 110s : those with yellow engine cowlings are Junkers Ju 52 Transports.

Left: In a harbour in Greece lies the cruiser *Kilkis,* bought by the Greeks from the USA. As the caption says, "The superstructure of the warship rises fantastically above the water, a symbol to all those who put their trust in England"!

Right: A German Henschel HS 126 reconnaisance plane flying over Athens. The HS 126 was the German equivalent of the British Lysander.

Above: The Russian T 34 tank had a quick-firing 76 mm gun, diesel engines and sloping armour; it was probably the best all-round tank used in the Second World War. These three got bogged down near Tolotchin on the River Drut, a circumstance of which the caption-writer was determined to make the most: "The crews of these Soviet tanks carry maps of Germany with them, but they don't know their own country. The huge tanks, weighing 42 tons, tried to escape the German pincer movement but became bogged down in swampy ground. While the Soviet troops fall foul of the natural hazards of their own country the German advance continues, overcoming all obstacles."

Left: On 22 June, 1941, Hitler dramatically "tore up" the non-aggression treaty which his Foreign Minister, Ribbentrop, had signed in August, 1939, and invaded Russia. The attack, condenamed "Barbarossa", involved three main armies under Von Leeb, Von Bock and Von Rundstedt, on the north, central and southern fronts respectively. The caption simply says that the photograph was taken on the morning of the invasion of Russia while the infantry waited for the artillery barrage to lift.

Over: The Central and Northern Armies advanced in the wake of General Guderian's armoured panzer divisions. Then in command of all German armoured units, Guderian was one of the outstanding military tacticians of his day. Here an amphibious Mark III tank is seen crossing the River Bug. It carries a 37 mm gun.

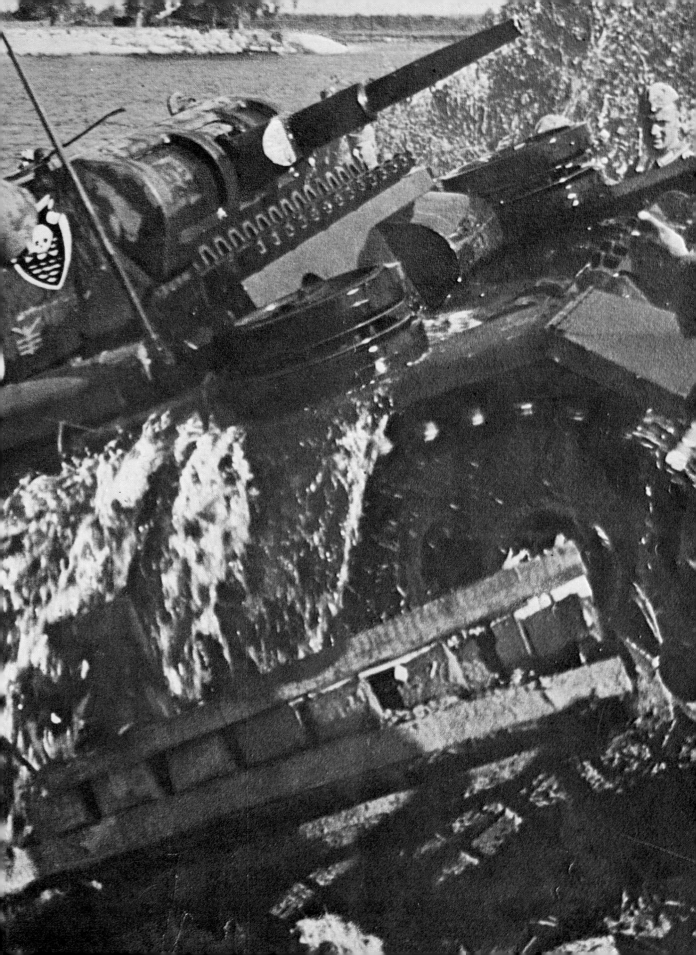

Left: Returning to Africa, *Signal* seems to be a little late with the news. While pictures of "Barbarossa" appeared in the July and August issues, this picture of General Rommel did not appear until September, yet the caption says that he is inspecting the ground after the battle of Sollum, otherwise "Operation Battleaxe", General Wavell's unsuccessful attempt to relieve Tobruk between 15 and 17 June.

Above: Just as photographs of Churchill were used by the British press as a symbol of the indomitable spirit of resistance and ultimately of victory, so these photographs of Hitler and Göring were intended to inspire faith in the Leaders of the Third Reich. The pictures were published at this time to mark the great success of the Luftwaffe on the Eastern Front, for which Göring was responsible. Göring who had been one of Hitler's 'cronies' from the earliest days of the National Socialist party, committed suicide in jail in 1946. It was he who coined the famous slogan "Guns before Butter" to encourage the German people to restrict consumption for the sake of rearmament.

The captions to these photographs show *Signal*'s ability to rise above the fact that the invasion of Russia was as callous and brutal an act of aggression as any in history. Instead one gets the impression that the Germans were there by invitation. *Signal*'s caption read "TWO DISTINCT WORLDS". Within sight of the advancing German troops, Soviet soldiers set fire to the houses of their comrades. As soon as they occupy a town, German soldiers take steps to prevent the homes of the people being destroyed by fire." Stalin did indeed institute a rigorous scorched earth policy and Russian troops were ordered to destroy everything in the wake of their retreat.

By September, 1941, when these pictures were taken, the Germans were 50 miles from Leningrad in the north, were east of Smolensk, were about to take Kiev and had advanced all along the River Dnieper in the south.

The top photograph shows German Mark IV tanks somewhere in Russia; the other two show street-fighting in the town of Zhitomir, about 80 miles east of Kiev. On the left is a German 10.5 cm gun, on the right a German Mark III tank.

Left: More propaganda — "The fantastic marching record of the German Infantry — some 70 kilometres (44 miles) a day — has shattered even the most optimistic estimates. Even a country as vast as Russia the German soldier takes in his stride. The depressing monotony of the interminable plains, the dogged resistance of the Russians, fatigue and bitter battles — nothing can deter the German soldier from his unshakable will to press on." This picture was taken near Vitebsk, about 280 miles east of the Polish border.

Above: November found the Germans 50 miles from Moscow on the central front and past Rostov in the south; but in the north Leningrad, under Marshal Voroshilov, remained defiant. The city was now into the third month of the epic siege which was not finally lifted until January, 1943. There is no clue as to where these pictures were taken but the caption indicates a certain lack of humour. It says, "'Here before you is what no animal could do.' This proud sentence might well describe the German soldier on the Eastern Front."

A Focke-Wulff FW 189 Reconnaissance aeroplane
flying over Finland. Early in 1939 the Soviet Union began
trying to extend her influence in the Baltic. Naval,
military and air bases were established in Latvia, Estonia
and Lithuania, whereafter various territorial demands were
presented to the Finns which they found unacceptable, as
a result of which, on 30 November, 1939, Russia invaded
Finland. The campaign that followed is known as the
Winter War and although the Russians, inevitably, were
the victors, all the laurels went to the Finns who fought
back with fanatical bravery, holding the Russians at bay
until March, 1940. In the event, Finland was obliged to
cede to Russia some 16,000 square miles of territory,
far more than had been demanded the previous autumn,
but she did, at least, retain her independence.

A German Military Band.

These two pictures, from the Eastern Front, appeared in
the December issue. In fact, by this time the Germans were
experiencing the full vigour of the Russian winter and the
Russians had started their counter-attack. In the south the
Germans had been driven out of Rostov and in the centre
Marshal Zhukov was driving back the troops attempting to
encircle Moscow. The German soldiers were not equipped
to face the cold and while fingers froze and rifles jammed
the Russians took advantage of conditions with which
they were all too familiar.

1942

On 7 December, 1941, a large Japanese Naval force, commanded by Vice-Admiral Nagumo attacked the US Fleet at Pearl Harbor just west of Honolulu and at once brought the United States into the war. Although perceptive observers realized that Germany could not possibly withstand the combined strength of Britain, Russia and America indefinitely and that victory was now only a matter of time, the new year found Britain in an atmosphere if not of despair, at least of gloom. The war in the Pacific rapidly spread across a front of several thousand miles and it was soon clear that the British forces in the Far East were totally inadequate to resist the Japanese onslaught. Hong Kong fell on Christmas Day and Singapore held out only until 15 February. 60,000 men were taken prisoner in what Churchill called 'The worst disaster and largest capitulation in British history'.

The tide of battle in North Africa was also on the turn. Although Tobruk had been relieved on 10 December and by Christmas British troops were back in Benghazi, on 21 January Rommel took the offensive and drove the British back to Gazala.

This page and overleaf: A remarkable series of photographs showing a German coastal patrol on the watch, the approach of a Bristol Blenheim bomber and its destruction.

Above: At sea the start of the new year held out no brighter prospects for the Allies than did the war on land. In 1941 the Germans had sunk $3\frac{1}{4}$ million tons of British, Allied and neutral shipping in the Atlantic. In 1942 that figure had been reached by the end of July. As soon as America entered the war Hitler diverted the spearhead of his U-boat offensive towards the east coast of America. The Americans were totally unprepared and suffered enormous losses.

Here a German cruiser is seen somewhere in the Atlantic.

Left: Rommel, as we have seen, had regained the initiative in North Africa and by 28 January the British had withdrawn to the Gazala-Bir Hacheim line. Thereafter little fighting occurred until the end of May.

The caption here reads: "SYMBOL OF VICTORY. In a German fighter squadron in North Africa, the custom has been introduced that before the planes take off against the enemy the flag must be raised. In this manner the German armed forces, so rich in tradition, combine the new with the time-honoured military customs." The aeroplane is a Messerschmitt Bf 109. The squadron emblem on the fuselage shows a panther's head superimposed on a map of Africa.

Right: When France fell in June, 1940, many Frenchmen felt that Marshal Pétain's decision to surrender to the Germans had saved them from a fate which might have been infinitely worse and as Germany's grip on the French administration grew ever tighter, not a few threw in their lot whole-heartedly with the enemy. Such a picture as this must have been very helpful to the Germans in convincing themselves, if no-one else, that far from being bloodthirsty aggressors they were indeed benign liberators. The caption reads: "SOLDIERS OF THE FRENCH LEGION. Fighting in German uniforms in defence of their continent and armed with German weapons (a Schmeisser Machine Gun) they have sworn fidelity to the Supreme Commander of the Armed Forces of the Third Reich. On the left (sic) sleeve of the nearest soldier are the colours of his country."

This series of photographs perfectly illustrates the "blitzkrieg" method of advance which the Germans had hitherto employed with such devastating success. But, ironically, in February, 1942, when these pictures were published the Germans were in retreat along the entire Eastern Front, although with the coming of spring the tide of war was to turn once again. The pictures show:

1. German infantry advancing through the fog, a German Mk III tank in support.
2. "The Infantry and the tanks — close co-operation between all branches of the armed forces is one of the secrets of German military success. The vanguard of tanks is supported by the infantry. The soldiers protect the tanks against Soviet guerrilla sharpshooters. The struggle against the hidden marksmen is extremely difficult, because the frost makes the construction of even the smallest shelter impossible."

3. "Tanks, infantrymen and engineers appear before Moscow. (At this time the nearest German troops were about 100 miles west of Moscow.) Here, where the snow conceals the presence of mines, the engineers move in with their instruments. Here we can see the co—operation between the three branches — the infantry fights the marksmen, the engineers fight the mines, and the tanks take on concealed enemy artillery."

4. "The village is taken and the tanks once again move to the head of the column. They will now launch themselves against new objectives, and with them march their comrades in the infantry."

Above: This photograph bears the eloquently brief caption, "At 35° below zero". By now the Germans were finding it increasingly difficult to keep the armies on the Eastern Front adequately supplied and were drawing dangerously heavily on their reserves of petrol. But in such conditions as this, it was impossible to stop them using up precious fuel in their efforts to keep warm.

Right: In the Atlantic a lone merchantman comes under fire from a German warship. By this stage of the war most merchant ships travelled in convoy, the efficacy of which system is borne out by the fact that of the 568 Allied ships sunk between January and July, 1942, only 53 were travelling in convoy.

Above: In March, 1942, when this picture was published the German spring offensive was still two months away. The caption gives no hint that the Germans have temporarily lost the initiative.

Right: A Tech-sergeant of the Luftwaffe. The badges on his collar are complementary to those on his shoulders. The yellow backing shows that he is a member of the flight-crew. The ribbon is that of the Iron Cross, second class. On his left breast is the Silver *Frontflugspange* (combat-sortie-badge) which was awarded to any airman who had flown 60 combat missions.

Left: A Lieutenant in an infantry regiment wearing the Knight's Cross of the Iron Cross.

Above: From left to right : Hitler, Keitel and Jodl. Field-Marshal Wilhelm Keitel (1882-1946) became Supreme Commander of the armed forces, responsible directly to Hitler, in February, 1938 ; in 1941 he assumed personal command of the armies on the Eastern Front. He was hanged as a war criminal in 1946. Colonel-General Jodl, who became Chief of the Operations Staff at German Supreme Headquarters, suffered the same fate. The insignia on his left-hand breast pocket show that he won the Iron Cross, First Class, in both World Wars.

German naval strategy in early 1942 was much affected by Hitler's curious obsession with Norway which, he believed, was to become one of the crucial theatres of the war. To this end he diverted much of his naval strength to the North Sea at a time when absolute command of the North Atlantic seemed to be within his grasp. As a part of this strategy he ordered Admiral Raeder to move the battle-cruisers *Scharnhorst* and *Gneisnau,* and the cruiser *Prinz Eugen* from Brest back to their bases in the North Sea. At midnight on 11 February the three ships left their anchorage and thanks to a brilliant feat of seamanship on the part of the German Commander, Vice-Admiral Otto Ciliax, sailed straight up the Channel and reached Wilhelmshaven on the morning of the 13th. The *Scharnhorst* had been severley damaged by mines but the *Gneisnau* and the *Prinz Eugen* were able to sail on to the Elbe. The elaborate aerial precautions taken by the British to thwart just such a break-out had proved utterly ineffective and the blow to British morale was considerable. Harold Nicolson says in his diary on 16 February, 1942, "I find that people are more distressed about the escape of the *Scharnhorst* and *Gneisnau* than they are even by the loss of Singapore."

These two pictures were taken in the English Channel on 12 February, 1942. *Above:* looking back at the *Scharnhorst* from the *Gneisnau* ; *Right:* Guns on the *Prinz Eugen* firing.

Previous page: A Messerschmitt Bf 110 over the North African coast. "'Onward to Victory,' says General Rommel," the caption tells us ; in reality there was very little action on the North African front in April, 1942.

Left: By May, 1942, the Germans had once again taken the offensive on the Eastern Front. They had seriously misjudged the harshness of the Russian winter, and in particular the effect that the seasonal deterioration in the condition of the badly made Russian roads would have on their motorized columns. Now, with the advent of milder weather, they were soon driving the Russians back along the whole length of the southern front from Voronezh to the Black Sea. This Russian anti-aircraft gun bears silent witness to the success of their spring offensive.

Right: In May the Germans also resumed their offensive in North Africa. This was a period of mounting crisis for the British in the Mediterranean, during which Malta was forced to the very limits of her ability, though certainly not of her will, to survive. The turning point came on 9 May when 60 Spitfires were brought in, whereafter control of Malta's airspace was gradually regained. In the face of Churchill's most vehement insistence, Auchinleck stubbornly refused to take the offensive in North Africa until he judged the moment right. After much wrangling Churchill gave Auchinleck the blunt alternatives of fighting or resigning, but in the event the choice became academic when, on 28 May, Rommel himself took the initiative and battle was joined. There followed six weeks of bitter and complex fighting at the end of which Rommel had driven the British back into Egypt as far as El Alamein and Tobruk was once again in German hands.

Here an Afrika Korps soldier scans the Libyan desert through a twin-lensed periscope.

Above: The caption reads, somewhat unhelpfully, ''An infantry soldier advances during an attack.'' He is carrying a Mauser 98K carbine and the date and uniform tell one that he was engaged in the German summer offensive on the Eastern Front. Once again the assault was successful and in the third week in July Hitler told General Halder, then Chief of the German General Staff, that in his view Russia was 'finished'. Rostov was recaptured on 23 July and the plan was then to strike south towards the Caucasian oilfields.

Right: August, 1942, and the Germans approach the grand climacteric of the war in Russia as they draw near to Stalingrad, the main objective of their autumn offensive.

Left: Field-Marshal Erwin Rommel (1891-1944) had been given command of the Axis troops in Libya, after the defeat of the Italian Marshal Graziani. At this point of the war he was at the height of his success, but illness, inadequate reserves and the arrival in North Africa of General Montgomery were to rob him of the final fruits of victory.

In July, 1944, he was badly hurt when his car was shot up by the R.A.F. Hitler already suspected him of complicity in the recent (June, '44) plot on his life and while Rommel was still recovering from his injuries Hitler offered him the choice of standing trial or committing suicide. Rommel chose the latter whereafter Hitler, with a lack of taste to which only the greatest criminals can aspire, accorded him a State funeral.

In this photograph he wears round his neck the Knight's Cross with oakleaf and swords, the *Pour le Merite* from the First World War and an Italian decoration.

Above: By September, 1942, the fight for Stalingrad had not only become the focal point of the German offensive in the east but had taken such a hold on public imagination throughout the free world that Stalingrad became at once the symbol and synonym of heroic resistance to a tyrannical invader. Here German troops are seen advancing towards the city, the outskirts of which were reached on 23 August. It had previously been heavily bombed and the Germans expected it to fall in a couple of days. The magnitude of their mistake can now be seen as one of the turning points of the war.

As *Signal*'s captions become decreasingly informative one must realise that the truth was becoming increasingly hard to tell. The caption to this picture simply says: "German anti-tank guns repulse an attack by Russian tanks." It was probably taken somewhere on the Caucasian front where the Germans were repulsed north of Ordzhonikidzhe and the threat to the Grozny oilfields was thereby averted. Further to the north-west the Germans had reached the Maikop oilfields on 9 August only to find that they had been destroyed.

*Left:*The caption says "Rumanian troops before Sevastopol" and appears in the issue for the second half of September, 1942, but one must go back to September, 1941, in order to trace the fortunes of war in the Crimea. In that month General von Rundstedt's drive to the Sea of Azov cut off the peninsula from the mainland and in October it was subjected to heavy aerial bombardment. In November, while winter immobilized operations further north, the Germans occupied most of the peninsula, taking Kertch and Simferopol but not Sevastopol. At the end of the year the Russians counter-attacked and re-occupied the Kertch peninsula. In May, 1942, the Germans regained the initiative and the Russians were driven out of Kertch once more. In July, at enormous cost to both sides,

Sevastopol finally fell and the whole peninsula was in German hands, this time to remain so until its final liberation in November, 1943.

The Germans had Rumanian, Italian and Hungarian armies fighting for them in Russia as well as a Fascist Division from Spain ; but their equipment was poor and since they could hardly be expected to show a very active concern in a contest between the Slav and the Teuton which was none of their making their numbers were by no means proportionate to their effectiveness.

Above: "A weapon which has no poet to sing its praises — the wire-cutter."

When last mentioned, Rommel was riding on the crest of the wave but in August, 1942, Churchill went to Cairo and as a result General Alexander took over from General Auchinleck and General Montgomery assumed command of the Eighth Army. Thereafter, from the Battle of Alam Halfa (30 August) to the fall of Tunis in the following May Montgomery never lost the initiative, although much hard fighting remained to be done. The caption for these two photographs reads simply, "Pursuing the Enemy." By September, 1942, "Fleeing from the Enemy" would probably have been more accurate. The guns are both M.34's.

Left: Field-Marshal Mannerheim (1867-1951) is one of the national heroes of Finland and was President of his country from 1944 to 1946. Having put up an heroic fight against the Russians in the Winter War of 1939-40, Finland at once sided with Germany, when Hitler invaded Russia in June, 1941. As a result, after a fruitless exchange of telegrams between Stalin and Churchill and Churchill and Mannerheim, Britain declared war on Finland the following December. This second act of Finland's participation in the war is known by the Finns as "The Continuation War". This picture was published to mark the 75th birthday of Germany's distinguished ally, and he is suitably bedecked with the Knight's Cross and the Iron Cross, First and Second Class, of both World Wars.

Right: The Germans remember their dead. Armistice Day, 11 November, 1942, some- where in Eastern Europe.

Another morale-boosting picture, the caption to which hardly reflects the situation in Russia at the time. "Tank 633 spots a Russian anti-tank emplacement and at once opens fire. Moments later the position capitulates and, the prisoners secured, the tank moves off to find new enemies." At about this time Field-Marshal Von Manstein, recently promoted to a new command called Army Group Don', made an attempt to break through from the south-west to relieve the German Sixth Army in Stalingrad. The attempt failed, largely because General Paulus, commanding the Sixth Army, refused to initiate a break-out from the beleaguered city on the grounds that Hitler had ordered him to stand and fight to the last man.

Left: On 19 November, 1942, the fate of the German Sixth Army at Stalingrad was sealed, when the Russians sent out pincer movements to north and south of the city and in three days completely encircled a quarter of a million enemy troops. Under the circumstances it is not surprising that *Signal* had to fall back on singing the praises of Captain Frantz who was a particularly distinguished officer of the *Großdeutschland* Division. He had been cut by a fragment from a hand-grenade, but nevertheless went on issuing orders to the assault gun unit under his command and displayed his imperturbability by smoking a cigarette. When the author of *this* caption was serving in an armoured car regiment the penalty for smoking a cigarette in an armoured vehicle was quite severe !

Right: Signal ends the year on a sunny note with a photograph of German infantry moving through maize fields in the Caucasus. The soldier nearest the camera is carrying an MG 34.

1943

That it is an artificial convenience to divide up books dealing with historical matters into annual segments is clearly demonstrated at this juncture. The new year was ushered in by no cataclysmic battle and the policies of statesmen remained as unaltered from the one day to the next as did the lot of the ordinary soldier.

If 1942 was greeted with discreetly-veiled gloom, it could be said that 1943 was greeted with discreet optimism, well watered with caution. Harold Nicolson headed his diary on 1 January, "I should like to feel that this is the year of victory, but I don't," At least he spoke of victory.

In North Africa Montgomery had won the Battle of Alamein in November, of which there is naturally no mention in *Signal,* and had driven Rommel back as far as El Agheila; while to the west the Americans, under General Eisenhower had landed in French North Africa. The Vichy French offered only token resistance and soon capitulated, whereupon Hitler rapidly sent in heavy reinforcements and the American advance ground to a halt near Medjez el-Bab.

On the Eastern Front the German Sixth Army remained bottled up in Stalingrad while in the Pacific the Americans, having landed on Guadalcanal in August, were finding the going very hard indeed. They were, nevertheless, on the offensive.

This, very briefly, was the situation as the war entered its fourth year.

Above: In the Atlantic the U-boats still had the upper hand. Churchill says, "The Battle of the Atlantic was the dominating factor all through the war. Never for one moment could we forget that everything happening elsewhere, on land, at sea, or in the air, depended ultimately on its outcome." It is hardly surprising, therefore, that *Signal* should greet the New Year with a photograph of a garlanded U-boat Lieutenant just back from a successful raid in the Caribbean.

Right: Putting a brave face on a not-so-healthy situation, *Signal* printed this photograph of a group of British prisoners-of-war in North Africa in its January edition, on the 20th of which month the British took Tripoli.

Above: A German bomber-pilot. The caption says, "In this, the fourth year of the war, our pilots attack the enemy with the same zeal as in the first."

Right: This picture must have been published at about the same time as the German General Staff were digesting the news of the surrender of General Paulus at Stalingrad. Manstein's attempt to prise off the Russian stranglehold had failed and efforts to supply the trapped army from the air resulted only in heavy losses of aircraft.

Paulus and his staff were captured on 31 January and by 2 February all resistance in the city had ceased. 90,000 men were taken prisoner ; they were all that remained of 22 divisions, more than 300,000 men.

At about the same time the Germans were also being driven out of the Caucasus, where this picture was taken. The caption reads, "The highest position of the war. German Alpine divisions have established fortified positions at a height of 4,200 metres in the Elbrus mountains, the dividing wall between Europe and Asia."

German Mark IV tanks passing a knocked-out British bren-gun carrier in the desert. The caption proudly states that : "These tanks are the latest in their series and are designed to be used in all sorts of conditions, from the freezing cold of the East to the scorching heat of the desert."

Left: A photograph of the Todt organization at work on the construction of the Atlantic Wall. Fritz Todt himself had died the previous year but his name lived on in the construction gangs by then recruited largely from slave labour imported from Eastern Europe. In the mid-thirties he was responsible for the construction of the Siegfried Line, the network of German fortifications opposing the French Maginot Line. It was for this task, which had to be carried out at great speed, that he originally created the Todt organization and the job was completed in a miraculously short time. Todt was also responsible for the construction of the Autobahns.

The Atlantic Wall was the name given to the coastal defences of France, Holland and Belgium. Alan Moorehead describes it thus: "The Atlantic Wall was a very formidable thing indeed. Every beach and cove was defended. Every seaside town was a fortress, with its seaward roads bricked up and guns sprouting out of the hotel cellars."

Right: Still the masters of the North Atlantic, U-boat men on the bridge.

Over: A fine picture of German capital ships on patrol in the North Seas.

Above: In the same issue appeared this photograph, the caption to which reads, "An American Boston Bomber has crashed to the ground in flames." It is in fact a Lockheed P.38 Lightning fighter.

Left: This picture appeared in the March issue of *Signal* on the 20th of which month the Eighth Army, advancing from the East reached Mareth, some eighty miles beyond the Tunisian border. On the other side of the country the Americans had run into trouble at the Kasserine Pass. This was their 'baptism of fire' in North Africa, and although they emerged victorious, it was an expensive and hard-won lesson.

The caption says "German troops land at a Tunisian airbase. The Grenadiers jump out and leave their aircraft at once." The aircraft is a Ju 52. Originally designed as a bomber, this three engine plane was obsolete as such by the time the war started but was used to drop paratroops in the invasion of Crete and throughout the war as a transport aeroplane.

eft: The caption simply ays, "Mortars hold part of n enemy garrison in heck, allowing an assault ection to move in." It is a cm mortar and the picture vas certainly taken on the Eastern Front to which the Germans had recently sent heavy reinforcements. Having been driven out of Rostov on 14 February and Kharkov on the 16th, they moved 25 divisions from Western Europe and launched a massive counter-attack on a narrow front in the Donetz basin. Kharkov was retaken and the front line was roughly back to where it had been at the end of 1941.

Right: "Italian cruisers weigh anchor to serve as escorts in the Mediterranean." The Italian fleet had actually played little part in the war at sea since November, 1940, when half of it was torpedoed at anchor in Taranto by British aircraft, and the other half was obliged to seek refuge in safer harbours. By this time the Allies had virtually regained control of the Mediterranean which had been lost to them after the German intervention in North Africa and had necessitated sending supply-ships 12,000 miles round the Cape to reach Egypt.

Above: A German Mark III tank in action on the Eastern Front.

Right: The Finns, as we have seen, had declared war on Russia immediately after "Barbarossa". Finnish troops are seen here fighting with the German armies on the Eastern Front. They seem to have appropriated the Death's head badge of the Waffen SS. The caption reads, "'Four minutes to go,' said the sergeant. The assault platoon of an illustrious Finnish regiment, moments before going into action."

Left: A group of German soldiers on the Eastern Front. The sergeant in the foreground bears the Knight's Cross and the Iron Cross. He also wears the Infantry Assault Badge, awarded for participation in six direct infantry assaults.

Above: During the spring and early summer of 1943 there was a comparative lull along the Eastern Front. Here a new engine is fitted to a German Mark IV tank. The gun is a short 75 mm.

Left: The Junkers Ju 87 has already been described. The caption simply says, "The bombs have been dropped and now the squadron returns to its flight formation."

Right: "A Grenadier attached to a tank battalion in the East. He has been there through two hot summers, two hard winters and dozens of battles." The machine gun he carries is an MG 42. Note also the mosquito net on his helmet. His belt-buckle bears the inscription *"Gott mit uns."* When R. S. Hudson, who was Minister of Agriculture from 1940 to 1945, was warned by V. V. Tilea, leader of the free Rumanian Movement in England, of what might happen if the Germans invaded Britain he replied "These things may well happen. But you forget that God is English". God clearly has his own racial problems.

Over: "The soldiers search the city house by house, protected by an anti-tank gun in the event of a possible counter-attack." There is nothing to tell one which city they are searching.

The Summer Offensive on the Eastern Front had originally been planned for the first half of May. It was then postponed until the second week in June and then again until the first week in July. During this time the Russians were well aware of what the Germans were up to and if the postponements did enable the latter to bring up huge reinforcements, it gave the former time to assemble an even more impressive show of strength.

The picture shows some infantry soldiers moving a gun limber.

Left: Throughout the war General Franco managed to keep Spain balanced precariously on the tightrope of neutrality. Though his sympathies naturally lay with his fellow Fascist dictators, his country had hardly begun to recover from the effects of the Spanish Civil War, which had only ended in March, 1939, and he realized that to provoke war with Britain would be to invite a naval blockade and effectively complete the starvation of his people. Hitler put considerable pressure on Franco to persuade him to let German troops pass through Spain to attack Gibraltar and the two dictators met for the first and only time at Hendaye, on the Franco-Spanish border late in 1940. But Franco would not be moved and Hitler said afterwards that he would rather have four teeth out than endure the ordeal of trying to bargain with Franco again. However, when Germany invaded Russia, Franco at once called for volunteers to join the fight against communism. Spanish soldiers are seen here boarding a train at Hendaye on their way to join the Blue Division, as it was known, on the Eastern Front.

Above: ''Fire on the Steppes'' says the caption. ''The wind spreads the flames across the path of the tanks. A rapid decision is called for — how best to avoid the flames.'' The tank is a German Mark III so presumably the Russians have set fire to the grass. The picture appears in the first issue for July, 1943, but as the German summer offensive, which was concentrated in the area between Orel and Kharkov, only began on 5 July it is unlikely that it relates to that.

Above: A good photograph of three Messerschmitt Bf 110s in flight . The shield on the side of the nearest aeroplane appears to contain a map of England !

Right: German troops had entered Bulgaria in March, 1941, and although the Bulgarian army was not used against the Russians and King Boris III remained on his throne until he died somewhat mysteriously in 1943, the country was in fact no more than a German satellite. Bulgarian troops were, however, used to suppress resistance movements in Greece, in Yugoslavia and in their own country. The caption says "The Bulgarian contribution to the fight for a new order. Bulgarian soldiers systematically eliminate partisan groups and restore order in their country."

Over: By the second half of August, when this picture was published most of the hardware in it was probably on the scrapheap. In the three major battles of that summer Kursk, Orel and Kharkov, both sides absorbed tremendous punishment, but by now the Russian war machine was in top gear and the limitlessness of their resources was beginning to tell. On the left of the picture can be seen the horse-drawn 10.5 cm guns. On the right, behind the half-tracks, are 21 cm guns.

eft: German torpedo boats travelling at speed. Note the
epth charges in the lower right hand corner of the
icture. There is no indication of where this picture was
aken but it is true to say that by the autumn of 1943 the
llies were once again masters of the sea. The Axis forces
n North Africa had surrendered on 13 May and the
nvasion of Sicily began on 10 July ; so not unnaturally
o pictures from that theatre appeared in *Signal* after the
March issue. It nonetheless left the Allies in control of

the Mediterranean ; while in the Atlantic the fortunes of
war were also turning in their favour.

Above: A Squadron of Focke-Wulff 190 fighters straight
from the factory. First introduced in mid-1941, and
powered by a 1,700 hp BMW engine, these planes had
a maximum speed of over 400 mph, were armed with two
20 mm cannon and two 7.9 mm machine guns and were
to give the allies a great deal of trouble.

U-boats setting out to sea. By this time U-boat losses had increased to a point where they exceeded their rate of replacement while, for the first time since 1940, new Allied tonnage surpassed the losses at sea. In May, 1943, forty U-boats were sunk in the Atlantic and at the end of the month Admiral Doenitz recalled the rest of the fleet to carry on the fight in less dangerous waters.

We must now return to the Mediterranean theatre, to which *Signal* has, predictably, made only the most cursory references in the last few issues. On 25 July the King of Italy sacked Mussolini and entrusted the government of the country to Marshal Badoglio. Mussolini was arrested and during the next six weeks was shunted around the country from one hiding place to another. In the south, organized resistance in Sicily ended on 17 August and on 3 September the Allies invaded the Italian mainland, whereupon Badoglio at once surrendered, although no announcement was made until

September 8. The Germans naturally regarded this as an act of treachery and took immediate steps to disarm or destroy all Italian units. The King and Badoglio fled from Rome and by 11 September the Germans were able to announce that Italy was now under their military control. Two days before, Allied forces had landed at Salerno, 30 miles south of Naples. The Germans had by now discovered where Mussolini was hidden and a raiding party under Colonel Otto Skorzeny was sent to rescue him. In spite of seemingly insurmountable difficulties, offered more by the nature of the terrain than the

efficiency of Mussolini's guardians, the raid was
successful and *Il Duce* was flown to Vienna. The first
photograph shows Colonel Skorzeny's paratroopers
getting ready to set out on *Operation Il Duce,* the second
shows Mussolini walking to the *Fieseler Storch* aircraft
which took him on the first stage of his journey. It is
interesting to compare this picture with the earlier ones of
Mussolini. As Major Mors, one of his liberators, put it "Now
he was an old and tired man, used up, visibly ill, with
hollow cheeks and unshaven, shaken by the events of
recent months."

Left: This young soldier carrying a couple of landmines does not do much to convey the state of affairs on the Eastern Front at this time. From Smolensk to the Black Sea, by October they had been driven back to much the same position as they had held at the end of August, 1941. The ribbons on his jacket show that he holds the Iron Cross, Second Class, and the *Ostmedaille.*

Right: The caption reads : "Forwards and Backwards. Marshal von Manstein and his aides study the map of operations." Although by this time it was nearly all 'backwards' and very little 'forwards', Field-Marshal von Manstein was nevertheless one of the most brilliant commanders in the German army. Basil Collier says this of him : "In this series of actions (the recapture of Kharkov, February-March, 1943) Manstein's performance as a master of strategy and major tactics reached its zenith. His shrewd judgement of Russian intentions, his preliminary dispositions, his refusal to be diverted by Hitler's impatience or the zeal of subordinates from what proved to be the right course, all stamped him as a master-craftsman whom few rivals either in Germany or in Russia could surpass."

1944

Once again the new year marked no turning point in the course of the war. The Allies were struggling hard in Italy, the Russian advance continued with ever-increasing momentum and as the German war-machine slowly ran out of steam so also did the presses of *Signal*. Since the first issue of April, 1940, two editions had appeared regularly each month. Now the month is dropped from the cover and the legend simply reads '*Signal*, Number One, 1944.'

In the Italian mountains, probably in the region of Castel di Sangro, German troops, incongruously dressed in solar topees, man an M.42 machine gun.

Left: The Führer. At a party gathering in Munich in September, 1943, he had announced that, however long the war might last, Germany would never surrender.

Right: Despite the devastating Allied bombing of the German aircraft industry, production still continued at a very high rate. Large factories were moved to rural areas and underground assembly plants helped to keep the wheels of industry turning. Here a line of Bf 109s nears completion.

Over: Another picture of the Atlantic Wall.

Left: Greece had been in Axis hands since April, 1941, and had suffered accordingly. In June of that year Germany handed over the administration of the country to the Italians, and in the first 15 months of this régime one-tenth of the population of Athens died of starvation. When Italy surrendered in September, 1943, Germany reassumed control. Irregular bands of guerrillas, known as *Antartes* had been busily engaged in sabotage throughout the occupation but they were divided among themselves and

much of their energy was wasted in internecine quarrels. When this picture of an assault gun passing the Acropolis was taken the days of the Germans in Athens were already numbered. The British re-entered the city on 14 October.

Above: German soldiers inspect the wreckage of a Soviet Sturmovik fighter which crashed somewhere on the Eastern Front.

The caption simply reads, "Going into Action." The snow
suggests that the picture was taken in the Northern part of
the Eastern Front where the Germans were being driven
back with less rapidity than in the south.

Left: "For two hours the infantry has stemmed the advance of the enemy by taking complete advantage of the terrain." This is the last issue for 1944 but there has been no mention of the Allied landings in Normandy.

Above: "The counter-attack presses forward" says the caption. One is not told where.

Doing its bit to keep up morale, *Signal* prints a picture of two test pilots and entitles it, "Their country before all else."

1945

This issue of *Signal* appeared in 1945 and as this
is a picture book and not a history book suffice
it here to say that Germany finally surrendered on
7 May and to end with as many brave faces as
Signal could muster under the circumstances.
The caption reads :"Our picture shows a group of
Luftwaffe helpers. Their eyes reflect the pride
which these young men take in their jobs. For
eighteen months now students have been taken
on as helpers for the air-force ; many have already
helped to scare off enemy aircraft. The red strip
on their epaulettes shows that they are volunteers".